A Vow of Purity: The Story of a Princess

Christina & Johnnie Johnson

Library of Congress Cataloging Data is available.

ISBN: 978-1-7354233-1-9

Dedication

We dedicate this book to our one and only daughter, Jeavonni Johnson aka "Ladybug". We pray that this book inspires her to obey God's word and to follow His Will for her life. We also pray that this book encourages her and all girls to commit to purity and follow God's rules so that they can marry the special man God created just for them. Remember, Jesus Christ is The King and Lord of all.

I am Jee Jee. My daddy tells me I am beautiful. When I look in the mirror, I feel amazing!

Daddy says I am a little princess and that I am a child of God.

I love playing dress up. When I dress up like a princess and stand in the mirror, I feel Royalty!

Daddy taught me to love myself and all of me. I love my hair, my head, my face, my smile, my body, and every part of me.

Daddy also taught me to respect myself. If I respect me, then everyone around me will respect me. I have to dress like a lady, walk like a lady, talk like a lady, and act like a lady.

Daddy always takes me on dates, and he makes me feel like a
Princess dancing at the ball.

One-day, daddy gave me a ring. I felt so special! I told daddy he couldn't marry me because he was married to mommy.

Daddy laughed and said, "This ring is your promise to save yourself until I give you away to marry the man God is preparing for you".

I said, "daddy I do, I do, I do!"

I do, I do, I do

Daddy sat me down and told me a story about how a princess can marry her prince.

Once upon a time in a high cloudy Kingdom, there was a King who sat on the Throne.

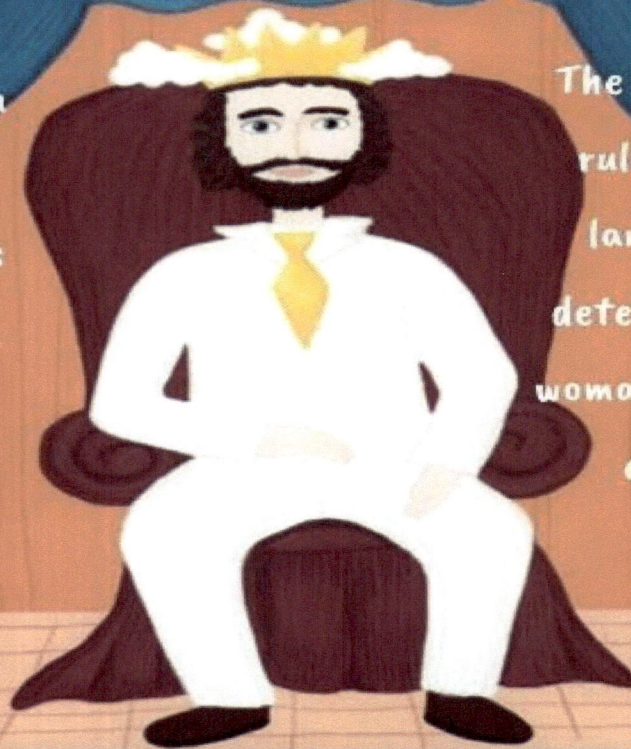

The King was the ruler of all the lands, and He determined which woman could marry each man.

The King handed out rules to all little girls, and only the girls who followed the rules could meet "the one" the King had for them.

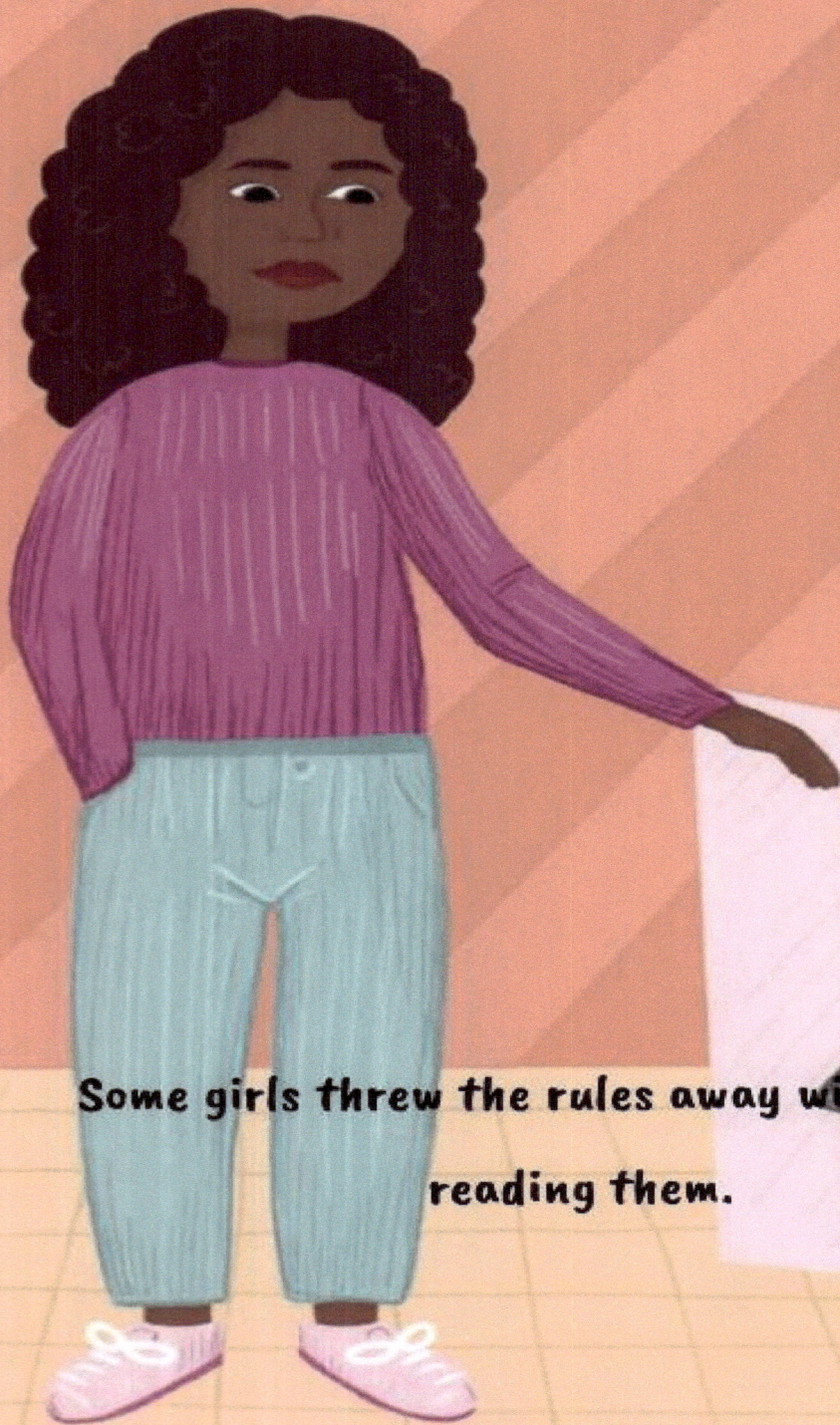

Some girls threw the rules away without even reading them.

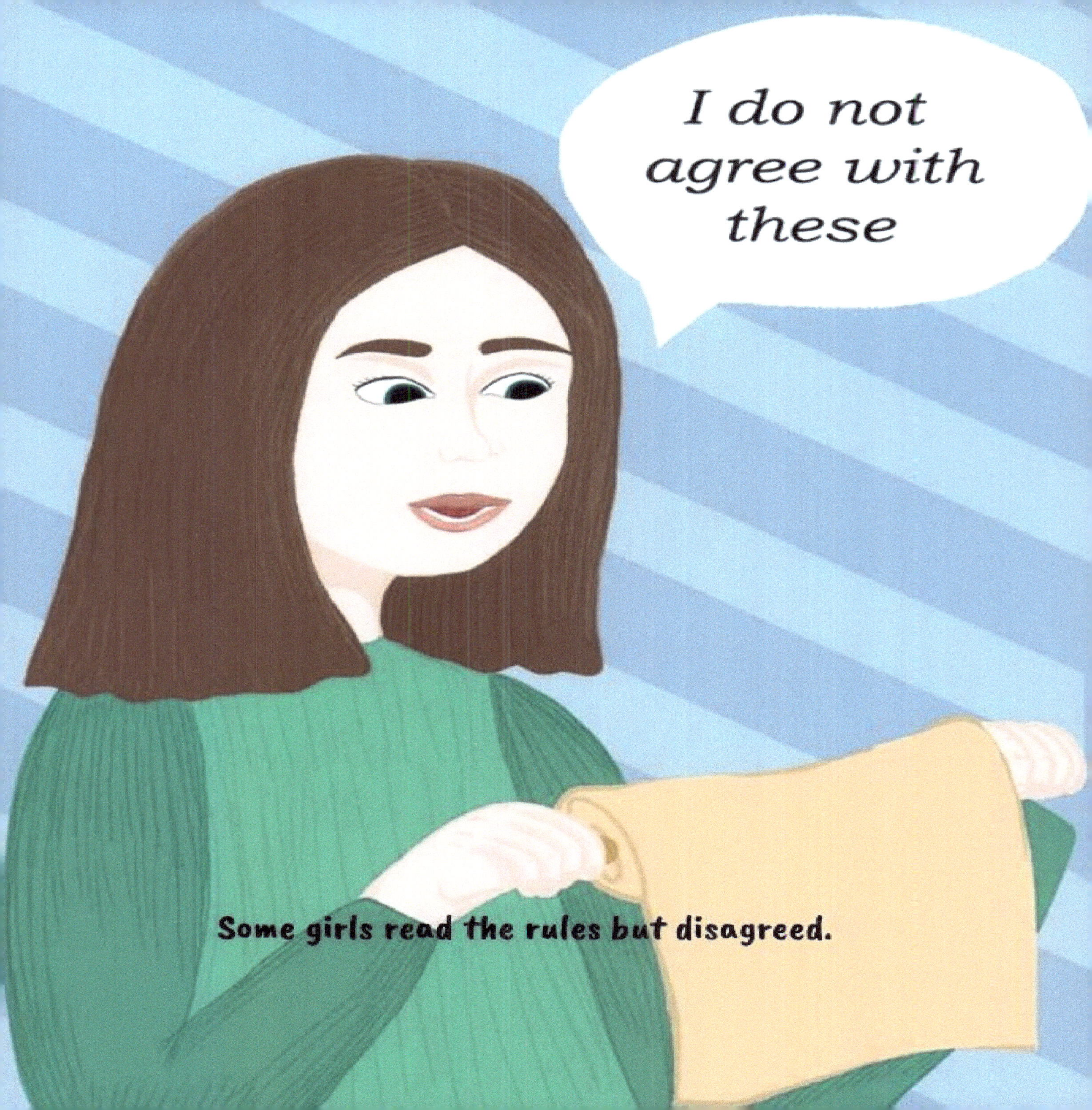

Some girls read the rules but disagreed.

Some girls thought they were too hard to follow.

Some girls refused to follow them.

What are your long term goals?

Some girls tried to follow the rules but failed.

All the girls struggled in some way as they all wanted to find the man of their dreams.

The rules were no secret because the boys had them too.

All of the boys struggled as they also wanted to meet their princess the King had for them.

The girls and the boys became confused, and all of them started to lose. The rules were not being used.

Some of those who didn't follow the rules still got married, but they walked down aisles without the blessing of the King. Those marriages were not built on a solid foundation.

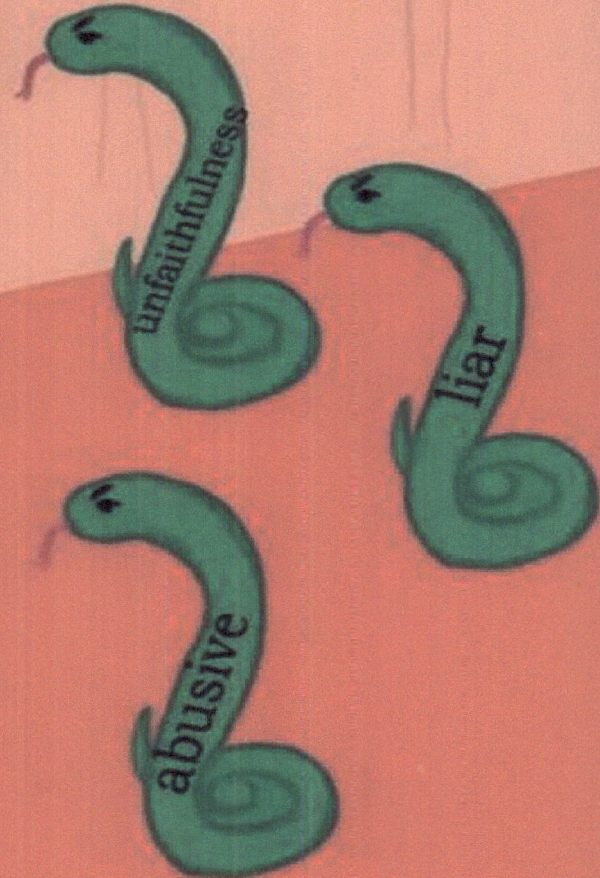

One girl, who struggled for years
without following the rules, wanted
another chance to start over.

She went to the King and asked for another chance to do things the right way. The King forgave her for her mistakes and He gave her a new copy of the rules.

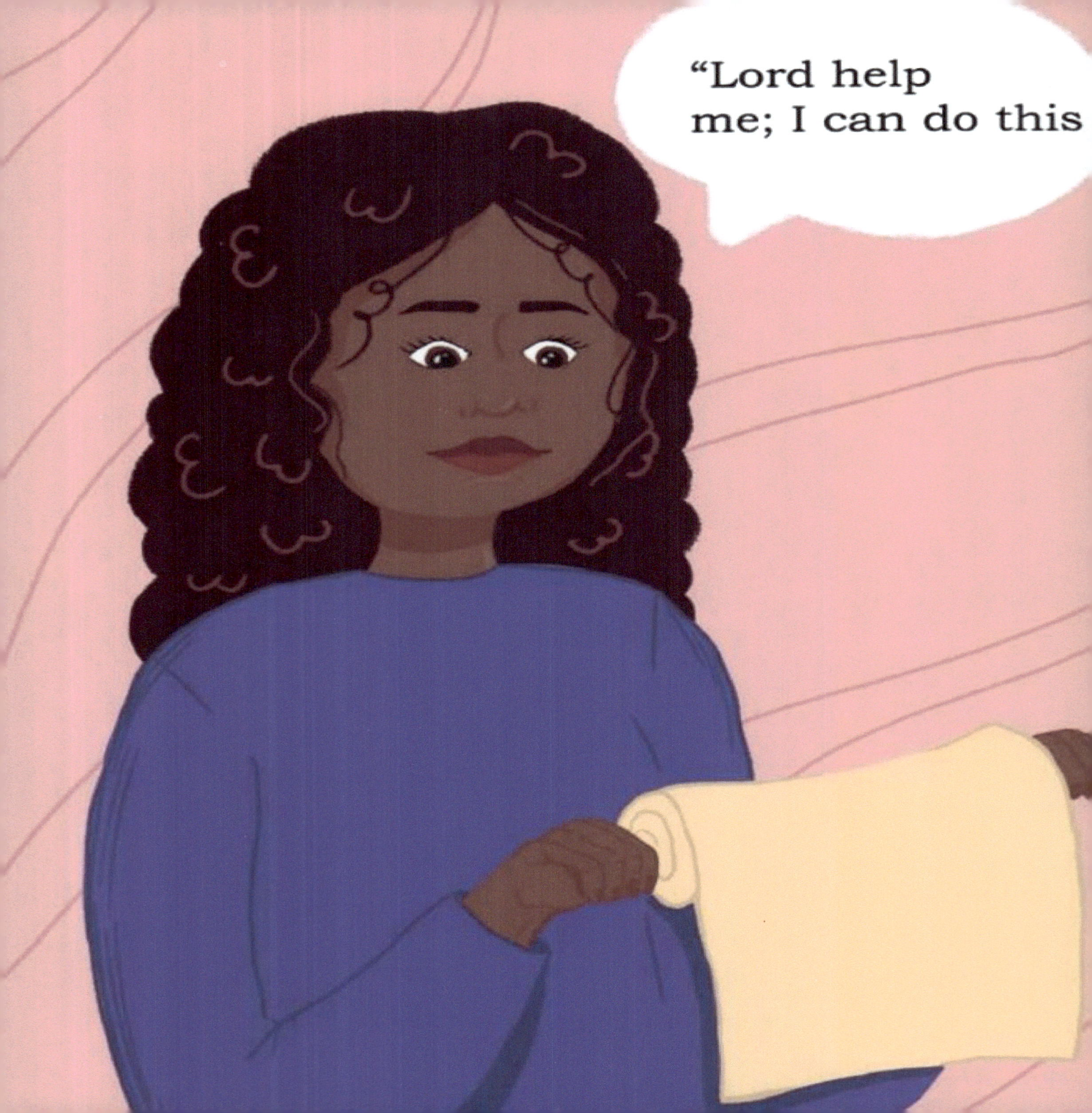
“Lord help me; I can do this

She focused on herself and honoring the King by following the rules.

The rules were simple:

Rule #1 Honor the King

Rule #2 Respect yourself

Rule #3 Vow to stay pure

Rule #4 Get to know the heart of a person to find "True Love".

Rule #5 Court and date for at least one year while pure.

Rule #6 Announce an engagement

Rule #7 Go Before the King to be granted a blessed marriage forever on your wedding day.

The King's rules provide the solid rock to the road that leads down the path to "the one" the King has just for you.

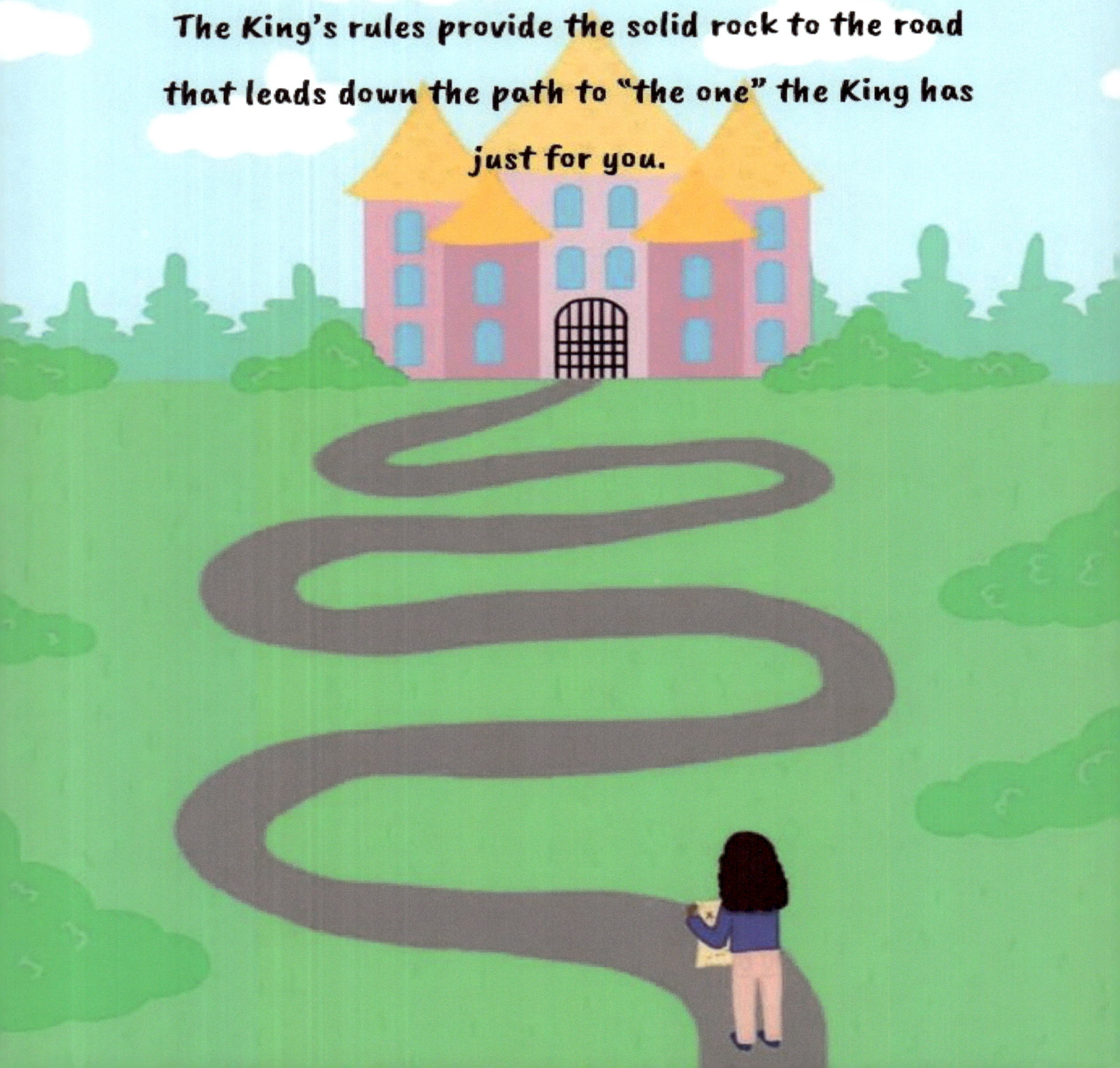

She followed the rules, and it did not take long.

The Prince found her, "the one", and she found

"True Love".

Her father gave her away on her special day, and
the King blessed them to live together happily
forever after as "one".

I gave Daddy a big hug and said, "Daddy, I'm going to follow the rules so you can give me away to my prince one day, but if I make a mistake, will you forgive me?"

Daddy grabbed my chin, looked me in the eyes and said, "ladybug, I will forgive you over and over again until you get it right, you will always be precious in my sight".

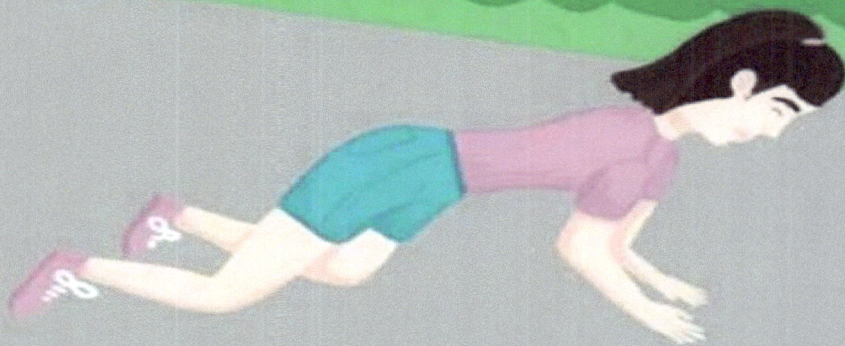

I smiled and said, "it's like a race. If you fall while running,

you can always get back up and keep running until you reach the finish line.

FINISH

Yet like the three little pigs, if you rush into building a house, it will not be made to last as a house built on solid rocks will last forever.

I said "I Love you too daddy"!

THE END

Scriptures every child should know:

Psalms 139:14 I will praise thee; for I am fearfully and wonderfully made.

Philippians 4:13 I can do all things through Christ which strengtheneth me.

James 1:17 Every good gift and every perfect gift is from above.

Jeremiah 29:11 For I know the plans I have for you," declares the Lord, "plans to prosper you and not to harm you, plans to give you hope and a future.

Proverbs 22:6 Train up a child in the way he should go: and when he is old, he will not depart from it.

Colossians 3:20 Children, obey your parents in everything, for this pleases the Lord.

Exodus 20:12 "Honor thy father and thy mother, that thy days may be long upon the land which the Lord thy God giveth thee.

1 Corinthians 13:13 And now these three remain: faith, hope and love. But the greatest of these is love.

John 3:16 For God so loved the world, that he gave his only begotten Son, that whosoever believeth in him should not perish, but have everlasting life.

Matthew 19:14 Jesus said, "Let the little children come to me, and do not hinder them, for the kingdom of heaven belongs to such as these."

1 Samuel 16:7   People look at the outward appearance, but the Lord looks at the heart."

Proverbs 24:16 For though the righteous fall seven times, they rise again

1 John 1:9 If we confess our sins, he is faithful and just and will forgive us our sins and purify us from all unrighteousness.

Proverbs 18:22 He who finds a wife finds what is good and receives favor from the Lord.

www.ingramcontent.com/pod-product-compliance
Lightning Source LLC
Chambersburg PA
CBHW042116040426
42449CB00002B/62

9 781735 423302